The First Human-Powered Flight

The Story of Paul B. MacCready and His Airplane, the *Gossamer Condor*

The First Human-Powered Flight

**The Story of Paul B. MacCready and His Airplane,
the *Gossamer Condor***

by Richard L. Taylor

Franklin Watts
New York / Chicago / London / Toronto / Sydney
A First Book

Cover photographs copyright ©: Comstock Inc./Bill Ellzey; Don Monroe (Inset)

Photographs copyright ©: Don Monroe: pp. 9, 41, 45, 46, 47, 51, 52, 53, 54, 55, 57, 58; The Boeing Company: pp. 10, 11; The Bettmann Archive: pp. 12, 13; The Royal Aeronautical Society: pp. 22 top, 30, 31; Comstock Inc./Russ Kinne: p. 17; Photo Researchers, Inc.: pp. 18 (Stephen Dalton), 36 (William Carter); The Drachen Foundation Archives: p. 22 bottom; Library of Congress: p. 26; Jay Mallin: p. 59.

Library of Congress Cataloging-in-Publication Data

Taylor, Richard L.
The first human-powered flight: the story of Paul B. MacCready and his airplane,
the Gossamer Condor / by Richard L. Taylor.
p. cm. — (A First book)
Includes bibliographical references and index.
ISBN 0-531-20185-6
1. Human powered aircraft—Juvenile literature. 2. MacCready, Paul
B.—Juvenile literature. 3. Gossamer Condor (Airplane)—Juvenile literature.
I. Title. II. Series.
TL769.T38 1995
629.133'34—dc20   94-44898
                                                                         CIP

Contents

Foreword

To Set the Stage . . .

Orville Wright made the world's first manned, powered flight at Kitty Hawk, North Carolina, in 1903. The airplane, named the *Flyer,* traveled only 120 feet (37 m) from takeoff to landing, but there were no balloons or gas bags to help, the airplane didn't glide downhill, and Orville had control of the airplane all the way. This flight was not something that "just happened"—the Wrights had researched the problems of flight and understood completely what they were doing.

Ever since, other inventors have claimed that they flew first, but none of them fulfilled the requirements of true powered flight. The Wright brothers' flight was the first time that a machine carrying a man had raised itself by its own power into the air, continued without losing speed, and was flown under complete control across level ground.

Human-powered flight must also be carefully defined to identify one flight as the world's first. This definition may be found in the basic requirements of the original Kremer Prize competition:

1. The aircraft must be a heavier-than-air machine (no balloons), powered and controlled entirely by its pilot.
2. The aircraft must take off from level ground in still air entirely by human power.
3. The aircraft must fly a figure-eight course with two turning points not less than one-half mile (.8 km) apart.
4. The aircraft must fly over a 10-foot (3-m) altitude marker at the starting line and cross the same marker again at the finish line.

These basic rules have been accepted as the definition of human-powered flight. There have been many short hops in airplanes and other machines propelled by human beings, but the *Gossamer Condor* is the airplane that met all the conditions and won the Kremer Prize. This was the first true human-powered flight.

The World's Biggest Model Airplane

In the mid-1930s, building model airplanes from kits was a popular hobby among young Americans. But these were not plastic models with parts that fit together perfectly—these kits had little more than a set of plans, a supply of balsa wood, and a tube of glue. The modeler had to cut each part from balsa wood, glue the pieces together, then assemble the airplane and cover it with tissue paper. It was very much like building a real airplane, except for the materials and the size.

Paul MacCready was ten years old in 1936 when he started building model airplanes. He wasn't satisfied with the models that came in boxes and was soon building airplanes he designed himself. These models weighed next to nothing—some of them, designed for indoor flying, had wings 3 feet (1 m) long but weighed only 1/15 of an ounce (2 g). The wings were covered with a clear, thin film, about the thickness of a soap bubble. Models like this were easy to repair after crash

Paul MacCready

landings, which happened often.

Paul MacCready was a very good model builder—so good that he won the National Junior Model Airplane Championship in 1941. He learned to fly a real airplane the next year, then became interested in gliders. He was good at that, too, and won several national championships. In 1953, Paul won the international soaring championship—he was the best sailplane pilot in the world.

Paul's model building, his three college degrees (two in physics and one in aeronautics), and his soaring experience prepared him well to lead a team that would design and build a human-powered airplane. The *Gossamer Condor,* which accomplished the world's first true human-powered flight in 1977, was very light, very fragile, and very easy to repair. It was a lot like a model airplane. Paul MacCready had learned his lessons well.

The Engine Makes the Difference

Bigger, faster airplanes that can carry heavier loads have been the goal of airplane designers and builders ever since the first flight.

Today, there are airplanes that weigh nearly 1 million pounds (455,000 kg) fully loaded. Supersonic transports fly routinely at twice the speed of sound. And the current record for weight lifted by an airplane is 329,000 pounds (150,000 kg).

The goals of size, speed, and load-carrying ability have been achieved and surpassed many times over the years. Improved materials, a deeper understanding of the technology of flight, and better ways of building airplanes have all contributed to this success.

But big, fast, heavily loaded airplanes can't fly without powerful engines to move them through the air. Airplane engines have grown from the homemade

12-horsepower motor in the Wright *Flyer* to jet engines with the power of thousands of horses. Bigger, better, more reliable airplane engines have truly been the key to progress in aviation.

This story is about another kind of airplane engine. Powerful? At its very best it generates only about one horsepower, and that for a short period of time, such as running up a flight of stairs. Reliable? It sometimes gets sick, and sometimes just doesn't feel like working. This "engine" is a human being, and although men have tried to fly under their own power for centuries, it wasn't until 1977 that true human-powered flight was accomplished.

The Boeing 747 is an example of the enormous airplanes that are possible today because of the powerful engines that have been developed.

In mythology, Icarus fell from the sky when he dared to fly too close to the sun, which melted the wax that fastened the feathers to his arms.

This is the story of the people who tried and failed, and the people on Paul MacCready's team who finally made the dream come true.

In ancient times (so the story goes) a Greek architect named Daedalus had a serious misunderstanding with his king—so serious that he and his son Icarus were thrown into prison on the island of Crete in the Mediterranean Sea. But Daedalus was too clever for his jailers. Using feathers fastened to their arms with wax, he made wings for himself and Icarus. Before long they were flying across the ocean toward home.

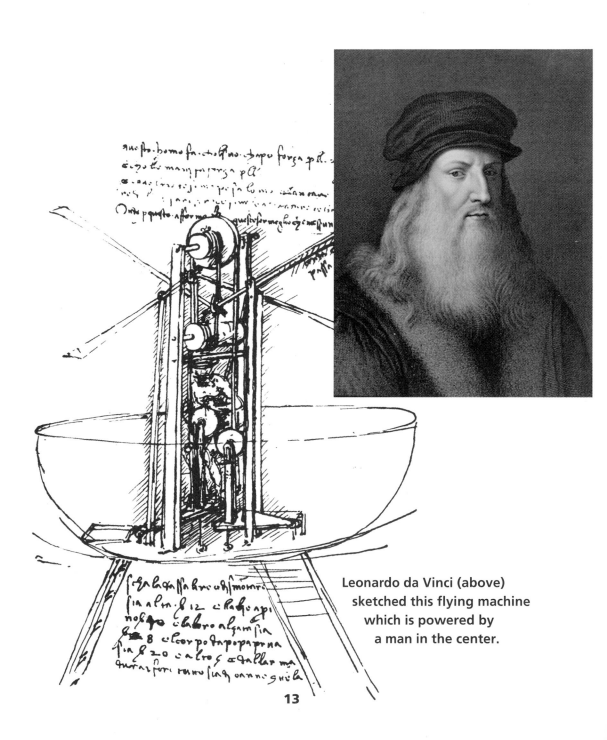

Leonardo da Vinci (above)
sketched this flying machine
which is powered by
a man in the center.

13

Unfortunately, Icarus was so excited about flying like a bird that he soared higher and higher. He finally got so close to the sun that the wax melted, the feathers dropped out, and he fell into the sea.

There were other flying legends as well, such as Sinbad, star of the *Arabian Nights,* who rode on the back of a huge bird called a roc.

Or you might consider Alexander the Great, another ancient aviator. According to legend, he harnessed a flock of hungry birds and dangled a piece of fresh meat in front of them. They pulled him through the air as they tried to reach the food.

Mercury was the messenger of the Roman gods, and he flew through the air, thanks to a pair of wings on each foot.

These myths and legends (they couldn't have happened except in people's minds) are examples of man's intense interest in flight. And they have one thing in common—all of these "flights" were based on flapping wings. It seemed reasonable that if the tiny muscles of a bird could produce flight, a man should be able to flap himself off the ground and through the air. Throughout history, people have tried to fly by flapping homemade wings. And throughout history, they have failed.

Even one of the greatest thinkers and inventors who ever lived believed that man could fly like the birds. Leonardo da Vinci, who lived In Italy five hundred years ago, observed eagles supporting themselves by beating their wings against the air and reasoned that a human could do the same: "[A] man with wings large enough and duly connected might learn to overcome the resistance of the air, and by conquering it, succeed in rising above it."

So Leonardo set out to design machinery that would allow a man to flap a large set of wings. He soon realized that arms alone weren't strong enough, so he sketched a machine that combined the strength of arms and legs. But the materials available at the time would have made Leonardo's machine much too heavy for human-powered flight.

Daedalus, Sinbad, and all the other fliers of legend and myth may have soared through the air in myths, but there was *something* that kept human beings from actually flying like birds.

Physical Limitations

Birds have evolved through millions of years into extremely efficient creatures. They do what they do very well, and bird flight can be divided into two major categories–simple and complex.

For example, soaring birds are simple flyers. They can literally float through the air for long periods of time without moving their wings. Sometimes seagulls seem to soar just for the fun of it (look for them playing hundreds of feet above the beach), but most of the time they're looking for food. True, they flap their wings like all other birds to get off the ground, but once they find rising air currents that will support them, they stop flapping their long wings and become gliders.

On the other hand, complex flight is well demonstrated by the birds that depend on catching insects for their food. Watch a barn swallow darting and zooming close to the ground as it chases gnats and bugs, and you'll see a real air show. With its wings almost

With their long
wings, gulls are
able to soar above
the water for long
periods seeking food.

constantly in motion, the swallow climbs and dives, reverses direction, changes speed, all in the blink of an eye.

It's important to realize that no matter how much a seagull might want to fly like a swallow, it can't be done. Gull wings are much too long and flap too slowly to accomplish the swallow's split-second maneuvers. And a barn swallow that tried to soar like a gull would find it very difficult as soon as its small wings came to a stop.

But all our feathered friends share several features that must be considered as we try to understand why men can't fly like birds.

The first is obvious: birds have feathered wings. A close look shows a light, strong wing whose primary purpose is to develop lift (the upward force that makes flight possible) when the wing is moved through the air. Each feather has tiny fasteners that act like zippers, allowing the feathers to spread out and catch a lot of

Sparrows are able to dart and swoop about quickly. The role played by the bird's feathers can be seen in the wings of this sparrow.

air when it's necessary, but holding the entire wing structure together.

Second, a bird's bones are thin and nearly hollow. Their strength is provided by lightweight braces on the inside. This combination of low weight and high structural strength is fundamental to any flying machine—whether it's a half-ounce (14.3 g) hummingbird or a 300-ton (273,000-kg) jumbo jet.

Third, other features shared by all birds are the relationship of muscle weight to body weight and the location of major muscles. Most of a bird's weight is muscle, and most of the muscle is concentrated in the breast. Those are the muscles that pull the wings downward and generate lift.

And fourth, birds are high-metabolism creatures. They expend a great deal of energy when they're flapping their wings, which means their hearts must beat very fast (as much as eight hundred beats per minute) to keep their wing muscles supplied with blood. Their breathing rate is likewise very high (up to four hundred breaths per minute) to provide enough oxygen.

There is no way that humans could ever adapt their bodies to meet these requirements for flight like the birds.

To begin with, sticking feathers in a layer of wax or tying them to one's arms wouldn't work, because the feathers would simply flop up and down. A bird's feathers twist and flex; they're an important part of the creature's flight-control system.

The human skeleton is composed of heavy bones with solid centers. They're stronger than birds' bones, but much heavier. Although humans have plenty of muscles, they are well distributed throughout the body. The most rigorous muscle-building program could never develop chest muscles strong enough to operate a set of wings. Even if that were possible, the new muscles would increase body weight, which would require larger wings, which would require more muscle, which would weigh more, and so on. A human being *might* be able to fly with flapping wings some day, if the wings could be made light enough and strong enough, but there's no solution in sight.

Early experimenters in human flight thought they could overcome these problems, and a lot of people were hurt trying to imitate the birds. If man were to fly using the power of his own body, it would probably be in a machine that didn't have flapping wings. The world would have to wait a long time for the materials and the knowledge that would make it possible.

The Secret Is Discovered

The great Leonardo and many others focused on flying machines that depended on flapping wings, no doubt because of their wonder at the flight of birds. For several centuries, inventors continued to come up with flapping-wing schemes, and "test pilots" continued to fail in their attempts to fly.

Hot-air and hydrogen balloons appeared late in the 1700s and indeed carried men into the air. But early balloonists had little control over how high they rose and absolutely no control over where they went. Ballooning was a far cry from flying like the birds.

It would take two major developments to unlock the secret of human-powered flight. The first of these was the propeller.

It began as a windmill, which turns slowly in the breeze to grind grain or pump water or make electricity. A windmill's blades are mounted at an angle so that the wind moves them. (You can see how this works by holding your hand out of the window of a moving car. Tilt the front edge of your hand just a little bit and the moving air will push your hand upward.)

In the thirteenth century, someone made a toy that used the principle of the windmill in reverse. Its blades were fastened to a wooden shaft which, when spun rapidly between one's hands, caused the whole thing to fly upward. (Toys like this are still available today.) If it were made much larger and turned on its side, and if the shaft were to be

Kites, such as these colorful examples, have been flown in various cultures for more than two thousand years.

turned by a strong motor, it could push (or pull) a machine through the air. The propeller was born. It was critical to the success of human-powered flight, because man is the only creature that can use rotary motion. Birds must flap—but man can pedal.

The second development was the realization that flapping wings were not only impractical for human-powered flight, they weren't necessary. This was proven by another toy: the kite.

For at least two thousand years before Leonardo's time the Chinese had been flying kites, and some of them were large enough to lift a man off the ground. A kite went nowhere because it could be flown only at the end of a string, but it demonstrated that whenever air flows over a suitably shaped surface, lift is generated. It doesn't matter whether the air or the wing does the moving.

A bird beats its wings rapidly up and down through the air to create lift and forward motion—the power is supplied by the bird's muscles. A kite remains motionless, pulling against its string, while the air flows around it and creates lift—the moving air supplies the power.

It wasn't until 1903 that the Wright brothers succeeded in putting all the elements together. In

December of that year, they made the world's first powered flight. Their airplane combined fixed (nonflapping) wings with a 12-horsepower engine and two large propellers.

The Wright brothers' accomplishment set off a flurry of powered-flight activity, and people lost interest in human-powered flight. By 1915, enough had been learned about building airplanes to produce a man-powered machine, but there was no use for such an airplane, and no one was interested. It would be many years before a prize was offered, a reward large enough to attract people who could build a successful man-powered airplane.

Getting Closer to the Goal

At the same time the first powered flight was accomplished, bicycles had become very popular. People rode bicycles for fun, but they also rode to work, to school, and even used bicycles to deliver light loads. Bicycles provided a transition between horses and automobiles, which had just been invented and weren't available in large numbers.

One reason for the popularity of the bicycle was its efficient use of muscle power. Its pedals, sprockets, and chain drive made it possible for people of ordinary strength to travel at relatively high speeds for long periods of time. With proper training, serious cyclists found that they could move faster and ride farther. The bicycle was a natural vehicle for moving a set of fixed wings through the air fast enough to get man off the ground under his own power.

In 1912, a French automobile manufacturer offered a prize for the first human-powered flight, but none of the contestants was able to get off the ground. After the rules were made a bit easier, the prize was won by Gabriel Poulain, a professional bicycle racer who managed to keep his bicycle-with-wings in the air for a distance of almost 12 feet (3.7 m).

To encourage the development of human-powered flight, a larger prize was then offered for the first person who could fly more than 32.81 feet (10 m) under his own power. Poulain spent the next ten years trying to win it. Success came in 1921 when Poulain, pedaling furiously on his "aerocycle," made four flights of nearly 40 feet (12.19 m).

But these were not really "flights"—they were more like long jumps. Without a propeller to provide thrust once in the air, the distance that could be "flown" depended entirely on how fast the bicycle was moving at the instant of takeoff.

Progress in motorless flight—gliders and sailplanes—continued during the 1920s. Stronger and

lighter materials become available, and more efficient designs resulted in new records for flight time without a motor. In 1922, a German pilot kept his sailplane (a very efficient glider) in the air for more than three hours.

The rapid development of gliders and sailplanes encouraged those who believed that human-powered flight would someday be possible. In 1926, two German scientists tested a group of highly trained cyclists, and found that they could maintain a steady output of 0.25 horsepower. With this information, a human-powered airplane could be designed to fit the "motor" instead of the other way around.

The first airplane designed for no other purpose than to fly with the power of a human being appeared in Germany in 1935. It was named *Mufli* (a contraction of the German word *Muskel-Flieger* for "human-powered flyer") and was built mostly of thin cedar plywood. *Mufli*'s 44-foot- (13.4-m) long wings made it look a lot like a sailplane, except for a 5-foot (1.5-m) propeller mounted on a pylon near the front of the airplane.

Despite its light weight (only 75 pounds [34 kg] without a pilot) and streamlined design, *Mufli* couldn't get off the ground by itself. A strong rubber cable was used to catapult the airplane to a height of about 10 feet (3 m), where the pilot would begin pedaling to keep *Mufli* in the air. The longest flight recorded over the next two years was 2,336 feet (712.5 m).

One of *Mufli*'s problems was the matter of "wing loading." That's an engineering term used to describe the number of pounds of aircraft weight lifted by each square foot of wing. If, for example, a 400-pound (182-kg) airplane has a wing area of 200 square feet (18.6 sq m), the wing loading would be 2 pounds (.9 kg) per square foot. And as wing loading increases, more speed is required to keep the airplane flying. *Mufli*'s wing loading was 2.35 pounds (1.1 kg) per square foot, which required more speed than a human could provide.

In 1937, a German engineer designed a human-powered aircraft using aluminum and other very light materials. It was never built, but the calculations showed that its wing loading would have been only 1.15 pounds (.52 kg) per square foot—less than half that of *Mufli*. This design was a major breakthrough and served as a model for many later attempts at human-powered flight.

The Kremer Prize

Progress in human-powered flight came to a stop during World War II as the aviation industry on both sides concentrated on bigger and faster military airplanes. But aircraft design and construction had improved remarkably during the war, and there were stronger, lighter materials available. In light of the new technology, a group was formed in England after the war to look for a solution to the problems of human-powered flight.

One of this group was Henry Kremer, a businessman interested in both aviation and physical fitness. He was told by the engineers and designers that a human-powered airplane was possible if someone would put up enough money for a reward. Kremer responded immediately by establishing the Kremer Prize for the first human-powered flight. When it was announced in 1959, the prize was worth almost twenty-five thousand dollars.

To win, the airplane would need to take off with no power other than that provided by the pilot, climb over a 10-foot (3-m) marker, fly a figure-eight course between pylons a half-mile (.8 km) apart, and climb over another 10-foot (3-km) marker at the end of the course before landing.

The lure of the Kremer Prize got human-powered flight projects going again. From 1961 to 1976, the

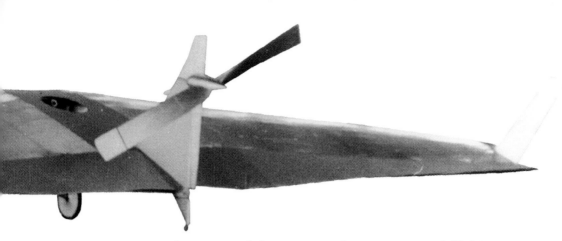

An array of unsuccessful attempts at human-powered flight: the English planes (top left) *Reluctant Phoenix*, (above) *Jupiter*, (left) *Toucan*, and (below) the French *Aviette.*

activity in England included an airplane called *Puffin* and another known as *SUMPAC* (for Southhampton University Man-Powered AirCraft). Both of these airplanes had wing loadings of less than 1 pound (.45 kg) per square foot and both of them flew—but not well enough to claim the prize.

The *Reluctant Phoenix* was another English design. It was an inflatable flying wing that weighed only 38 pounds (17.3 kg), but its best performance was a flight of only 420 feet (128 m), and the inventor gave up.

The Kremer Prize was originally intended for British citizens only, but was expanded in 1967 to include competitors anywhere in the world. In Japan, a group of advanced aeronautical students built several human-powered airplanes. They were all named for birds, among them the *Linnet,* the *Egret,* and the *Stork.*

Back in England, one team tried to overcome the power problem by building a two-man airplane. Its name was *Toucan* (Two Can Fly if One Cannot), its wings measured 123 feet (37.5 m) from tip to tip, and its longest flight was 2,100 feet (640.5 m) at an altitude of 15 feet (5 m).

The French-built *Aviette* had 132-foot (40.3-m) wings and a very low wing loading of 0.51 pounds (.23 kg) per square foot. It flew in a straight line for a distance of 3,281 feet (1,000.7 m), but was so delicate that it could barely be turned.

All of these airplanes were very well designed and beautifully built. They all got off the ground and flew, some for short hops, some for considerable distances. But they all suffered from the same problems—they were either too heavy, or they were limited to straight-line flight.

Henry Kremer was aware that none of the human-powered airplanes built since 1959 had even come close to flying the figure-eight course. He was so interested in seeing the prize won that in 1973 he raised the award to £50,000—at that time, about $129,000.

The larger prize resulted in several new designs in France, England, and Japan, and a slow but steady increase in distance flown. An English airplane named *Jupiter* flew 3,513 feet (1,071.5 m) in 1972. This was a new world record but still not enough to win the Kremer Prize.

In 1973, a group of students at the Massachusetts Institute of Technology built a lightweight two-winged airplane to be powered by two men. They named their creation *Burd,* and although it never flew, it was the first indication of serious interest in human-powered flight in the United States.

It was another three years before an American left the ground under his own power. In April 1976, Joseph A. Zinno powered and piloted his *Olympian ZB-1* for a distance of 77 feet (23.5 m) at an altitude of 1 foot (.3 m).

There were other human-powered projects under development, but in 1976 Zinno's short flight was America's best effort. That would change soon, because another very talented American decided to enter the race.

Lightweight and Big Wings

In the summer of 1976, Paul MacCready got serious about human-powered flight. It was a family project from the start, especially for his sons, who became important members of the team that won the Kremer Prize. Paul knew that their involvement in a project like this would teach them things they could never learn in school.

In addition to powered airplanes and sailplanes, Paul and his sons had tried hang gliding, in which the pilot is suspended below a kitelike glider and controls it by shifting his weight.

Like any other glider, a hang glider is constantly falling through the air, using gravity for its "power" and trading altitude for forward motion. If the pilot finds air that is rising faster than the glider is sinking, he can stay aloft for long periods of time and glide long distances.

Wing loading becomes very important. A flight glider with large wings (and therefore low wing loading)

will stay in the air longer and glide farther. It's also possible to calculate the amount of "power" a glider uses to move through the air. In the case of human-powered flight, the power generated by the pilot would be used to maintain level flight instead of falling through the air.

Paul studied this closely and determined that a lightweight glider with very large wings could probably be flown with less than one-half horsepower. How light must it be? He figured that the airplane should weigh no more than half its pilot's weight—probably not more than about 80 pounds (36 kg). How large must the wings be? Paul wasn't concerned about how the airplane would look, only that it could develop enough lift to fly at very low speeds. And that would require a wingspan of nearly 100 feet (30 m). The wing loading should be no more than 0.25 pounds (.03 kg) per square foot.

Paul MacCready knew that a champion bicycle racer could produce a half-horsepower, he was sure he could build an airplane light enough and large enough, and so he decided to enter the race for the Kremer Prize. He had established the principle that would govern his team—"we know it can be done, now let's just do it!"

First he built a model to test his theory. It was little more than a wing 8 feet (2.4 m) long, braced above and below with thin wires, and having the same wing loading he had calculated for the full-size airplane. Up-and-down movement of the nose would be controlled by a canard (a small second wing) mounted on a boom in front of the main wing. The pilot's weight would act like a pendulum and provide stability, just like a hang glider.

Test glides showed that the model needed a larger canard. When that change was made, the model flew well enough to convince Paul that his ideas were sound and that the world's first human-powered flight was a project worth continuing.

A One-of-a-Kind Flying Machine

Most of the human-powered airplanes that had managed to struggle off the ground by 1976 looked like streamlined sailplanes. Their long, narrow wings very efficient, but they were so long they had to be braced internally. That added a lot of weight, perhaps enough to keep these airplanes from flying successfully.

Paul MacCready and the team he assembled in California never considered internal bracing. Their goal was to build a "flying wing" that weighed as little as possible; that meant it would be a wing braced by many thin wires on the outside. At normal airplane speeds, those wires would create enough drag to prevent flight, but this airplane wasn't normal—it would fly very slowly, and the wires wouldn't cause a problem.

The original plans showed the influence of Paul's hang-glider studies. The main spar for the wing was an aluminum tube 88 feet (27 m) long and 2 inches (5 cm) in diameter. Seven aluminum ribs attached to the spar gave the upper surface of the wing a curved shape so it would develop lift more efficiently at low speeds. Another aluminum tube served as the keel, supporting the propeller in the rear and the canard out front.

The basic structure was completed by two vertical aluminum tubes that provided anchor points for the bracing wires and support for the pilot's seat. The wires on top kept the wings from collapsing on the ground, and the lower wires raised the entire airplane when the wings developed lift.

The most striking thing about this strange airplane was its skin. Most normal airplanes are covered with thin sheets of aluminum, but a metal skin was far too heavy to be considered for this one. Most of the other competitors for the Kremer Prize covered their airplanes with lightweight fabrics, but even that wasn't light enough for the MacCready team. They used a clear, super-thin polyester film called *Mylar,* a material much like the tape used in audiocassettes. It was extremely light and shrank a bit when heated to make a tight, smooth surface.

Early in September 1976, as the airplane took shape in a large rented building in Pasadena, the team searched for a name for their airplane. They were inspired by the California condor, a near-extinct soar-

Paul MacReady and his team work on the thin mylar covering of the *Gossamer Condor*.

ing bird with 9-foot (2.75-m) wings that lives in the Sierra Nevada mountains. The word *gossamer* means light, filmy pieces of cobweb floating in the air and was a perfect way to describe the fragile airplane they were building. And so the biggest model airplane in the world became the *Gossamer Condor*.

The first "flight," which was just a test to find out if the airplane would lift itself off the ground, took place on the night of September 14, 1976, in an empty parking lot. Lines were fastened to the *Condor,* and it was pulled across the ground at about 5 miles (8 km) per hour. The air flowing over the curved plastic skin generated enough lift to make the airplane tug against the lines—the *Condor* tried to fly!

Then, disaster. As the fragile airplane was being moved indoors after the test, a gust of wind struck it and the right wing buckled. Other parts of the frame began to fall, and within a few minutes, the *Gossamer Condor* had collapsed into a heap of aluminum tubing, wire, and plastic film. Even though the airplane hadn't actually flown, Paul MacCready was satisfied that his design would work.

He decided to pick up the pieces and move ahead.

Two New Homes, New Ideas, and an Engine

After the initial flight tests, the *Gossamer Condor* project was moved to the Mojave Airport, located in the desert 75 miles (120 km) north of Los Angeles. There was a big hangar in which to rebuild the *Condor* and plenty of open space to conduct flight tests and, hopefully, try for the Kremer Prize.

As the new airplane took shape, two words guided the MacCready team—every part had to be *light* and *strong* as possible.

For example, the main wing spar was made from 12-foot (3.7-m) sections of aluminum tubing with walls only .0035 inch (.9 mm) thick. But that wasn't light enough, so the tubing was chemically milled (using chemicals to etch, or eat away, unneeded aluminum) until the walls were no thicker than a staple. When it was finally put together, the wing spar resembled a 95-foot- (29-m) long aluminum soft-drink can.

The rest of the *Condor* was just as flimsy. If the wires were tightened a bit too much, one part might buckle or collapse, putting too much load on another piece of the structure, and it would fall. This happened over and over again, but the lightweight materials were easy to repair or replace, and the airplane would be ready for another test in a short time.

On the other hand, each crash was an opportunity to rebuild and improve the airplane. If a part never broke, it might be too strong or too heavy. So each time something failed, it was replaced with something better—the failures actually resulted in the lightest, strongest airplane possible.

The "engine compartment" had a lightweight bicycle seat and a back support for the pilot. The pedals were mounted directly on the bottom vertical post, and a lightweight chain transmitted the pilot's power output to the propeller shaft overhead.

This was different from most of the other airplanes in the Kremer competition, because their pilots "bicycled" along the ground until the airplane was moving fast enough to fly. Paul figured that the *Condor* would be able to take off from a standing start using the propeller alone. So two small plastic wheels—the kind used on toy trucks—were used instead of bicycle wheels, which were much heavier.

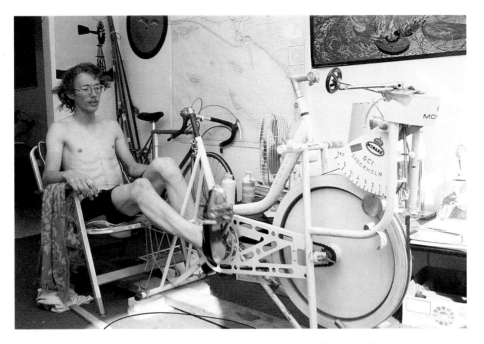

Pilots of the *Gossamer Condor* built up their cardiovascular endurance and leg strength by training on an ergometer.

The *Condor's* "engine" also had to be light and strong. Paul MacCready and his two teenage sons built up their strength on an ergometer, a stationary bicycle that measures horsepower. On the day after Christmas 1976, Parker MacCready flew the *Condor* in a straight line for 40 seconds, covering 469 feet (143 m) at a height of 3 feet (1 m). Parker was exhausted, but it was the first time the airplane had flown more than a few feet. Unfortunately, the Kremer Prize would require at least seven minutes of flight and two turns—the *Condor's* "engine" would have to be much stronger.

Greg Miller, a championship-competition bicyclist, sits in the "cockpit" of the *Gossamer Condor* awaiting a test flight.

On January 2, 1977, the Japanese team competing for the Kremer Prize flew their *Stork* 6,870 feet (2,095 m) on a four-and-half-minute flight. That was the distance Paul had figured would be necessary to win the prize, but like the *Condor,* the *Stork* was difficult to turn. Nevertheless, MacCready knew that he'd have to come up with a better engine, and soon.

The solution was eighteen-year-old bicycle racer Greg Miller. He was not a pilot, but he learned quickly, and by the end of January he had flown the *Condor* farther and higher than anyone else.

The biggest problem during the test flights was the turbulent air at Mojave, caused by the winds that frequently howled across the desert. Even the slightest disturbance in the air made the wings twist and change shape, often making it impossible for Miller to keep the *Condor* in the air.

This flight in March 1977 ended in a crash that sent the *Gossamer Condor* back to the hangar for rebuilding.

Something had to be done, and Paul made the decision to move again to escape the wind. The *Condor*'s parts and pieces were packed up and taken to Shafter Airport, in the San Joaquin Valley, near Bakersfield, California. There were not many airplanes at Shafter, and there was very little wind—perfect conditions for the *Gossamer Condor*.

The move to Shafter Airport was a good time to rebuild the airplane, and within two weeks a new and improved *Gossamer Condor* stood in the hangar. The wings were narrower at the tips, the Mylar skin now covered the bottom surfaces of the wings as well as the tops, and there was a streamlined, enclosed cockpit for the pilot.

This airplane was the twelfth major change in the original *Condor* design, and in all but the smallest details, it was the airplane that Paul MacCready knew could win the prize. He was so confident of success that he painted two big Xs on Shafter's north-south runway to mark the turning points for the Kremer Prize course.

The first chance to fly the new airplane came on March 4. Eleven-year-old Tyler MacCready was the pilot, and he made six short flights that evening. The new *Condor* was much easier to fly, until Tyler tried to change its direction. Maybe Greg Miller, with more muscle, would be able to make it fly.

On March 6, after several short flights, Greg pedaled as hard as he could, and flew the *Gossamer Condor* in a straight line for five minutes and five seconds. It was the longest human-powered flight in history, but the turning problem wouldn't go away.

When an airplane is flying straight ahead, the wings are level and all of the lift acts straight up. But if the airplane rolls, or banks, some of the lift begins to act in a horizontal direction. This is the force that actually pulls an airplane around a turn.

Most airplanes are banked by the action of ailerons (a French word that means "little wings"). These are small, hinged portions of the trailing edges of the wings. When the pilot moves the control, one aileron goes up, the other goes down. This changes the airflow over that part of the wing, causes one wing to develop more lift than the other, and the airplane banks.

But ailerons wouldn't work on the *Condor*. There were problems of stability and control that no one had encountered before, because no one had ever tried to fly such a big, light, and slow airplane. Paul MacCready and his team were exploring a completely new realm of flight.

They also tried to warp, or twist, the wings to create more lift on one side, thereby banking and turning the

Condor. (Wing warping worked for the Wright brothers' first airplane, which had much shorter wings.) But that didn't solve the problem, either. The wings were simply too long and the airplane too light to be banked using normal controls.

Tyler MacCready stumbled on the solution during a flight on April 5. He moved the control to twist the wings, but he moved it in the opposite direction. The twisted-down wing created enough drag to act as a brake that swung the *Condor* around in a beautiful turn. "Reverse warping" solved the turning problem, and the MacCready team now knew they could win the prize.

While all this was going on, Greg Miller announced that he intended to leave for Europe to compete in a professional bicycle race. The *Gossamer Condor* was once again an airplane without a pilot.

The replacement pilot was Bryan Allen, a twenty-three-year-old amateur bicycle racer who was also a fine hang-glider pilot. He was a roommate of one of the team members and had been helping out as a wing-walker. Bryan jumped at the chance to be the pilot, made his first flight in the *Condor* on April 7, and was soon able to make the airplane turn under complete control.

Part of the *Gossamer Condor* team: (from left) Paul MacReady, Bryan Allen, Tyler MacCready, Vern Oldershaw, and Jim Burke.

By the end of May, the *Gossamer Condor* had made more flights than all the other Kremer competitors combined, but it still couldn't fly far enough or make the turns required for the Kremer Prize. A different wing was designed and built, but it didn't improve the airplane's performance.

The culprit was the Mylar wing covering. Whenever it became loose enough to quiver and change its shape, drag increased so much that Bryan's hardest pedaling couldn't overcome it. The problem was solved by heating the Mylar very carefully with hair dryers, causing the skin to shrink and pull the entire surface tight and smooth.

All through June and most of July the tests continued, with small changes between flights. A new canard with a slightly different shape made a big improve-

ment, and on August 4, Bryan flew for 7 minutes. That flight was an official attempt, and would have won the Kremer Prize if one of the wheels hadn't touched the T-bar that marked the first 10-foot (3-m) hurdle.

On August 6, the *Condor* team tried again. Halfway around the course, a pulley in the canard control came loose and the airplane crashed to the runway. It took eleven days to repair the damage.

On August 20, Bryan flew the entire figure-eight course, but without climbing to the required altitude. It was the first time that anyone had actually flown the figure-eight Kremer course, and it was the longest flight in the history of human-powered airplanes.

Gusty winds prevented any more attempts until August 22. On that Monday morning, when Bryan got to the halfway point on the first leg of the figure-eight, the wind changed direction and increased in strength. The

Not only did the *Gossamer Condor* need to complete the figure-eight course, it also had to climb to a regulation height.

flight time was 7 minutes and 22 seconds, but Allen had used up so much energy because of the wind that the *Gossamer Condor* couldn't clear the 10-foot (3-m) marker at the end of the course. They didn't win the prize that day, but MacCready and his team knew they could do it—if only the wind would cooperate.

At 7:25 A.M. the next morning, August 23, the wind was blowing only 2 miles (3.2 km) per hour, and Paul decided to make another attempt. Bryan took off to the north at exactly 7:30 A.M., cleared the first marker with 2 feet (.6 m) to spare, and started out on the figure-eight course. Team members rode alongside on bicycles coaching Allen, telling him when to climb, when to start turning, shouting encouragement.

The turn around the first pylon cost the *Condor* 10 feet (3-m) of altitude, and Bryan regained 1 foot (.3 m) on the southbound leg of the course. Once again the

Two views of the *Gossamer Condor* on its way to winning the Kremer Prize for the first successful human-powered flight.

wind shifted, but Allen pedaled harder, and the *Gossamer Condor* soared over the 10-foot (3-m) T-bar marking the finish line. Bryan could have landed straight ahead, but he kept flying for almost 300 feet (91.5 m), made a half-right turn, and brought the *Condor* gently to earth on the centerline of the course.

The Kremer Prize had finally been won. The first human-powered flight was in the record books.

After the Prize

Several days after the prizewinning flight, team members were invited to fly the airplane as a reward for their efforts and interest in the project. On September 22, the *Gossamer Condor* was flown by Maude Oldershaw. A sixty-year-old grandmother and a pilot, she was the first woman in the world to fly a human-powered airplane.

The success of the human-powered flight project was truly a team effort. When Bryan Allen shouted, "We did it!" at the end of the Kremer flight, he was referring to all the people whose knowledge, dedication, and hard work made the project possible.

Throughout the *Gossamer Condor*'s development, the MacCready team was making history—no one had ever tried to build an airplane quite like this. Their work advanced the frontiers of discovery and resulted in new applications of low-power transportation. Thanks to Henry Kremer's foresight and the prize he

The lighter and stronger *Gossamer Albatross* won another prize sponsored by Henry Kremer by flying across the English Channel in 1979.

sponsored, the world was changed a bit for the better.

Two years later, Paul MacCready and his associates built a lighter, stronger human-powered airplane called the *Gossamer Albatross*. On June 12, 1979, they won another prize sponsored by Henry Kremer, this time for flying across the English Channel. The pilot was Bryan Allen, and he made the 22.25-mile (35.6 km) trip in 2 hours and 49 minutes.

Shortly after the *Gossamer Condor's* prize-winning flight, the airplane was accepted for display in the Smithsonian Institution's National Air and Space Museum in Washington, D.C. It remains there as a permanent exhibit, hanging in a place of honor with the Wright *Flyer* and the *Spirit of St. Louis,* two of the many "firsts" that have made America so prominent in aviation history.

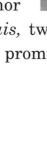

SITE OF GOSSAMER CONDOR FLIGHT

THIS PLAQUE AT SHAFTER AIRPORT COMMEMORATES THE WORLD'S FIRST MAN-POWERED FLIGHT TO COMPLETE THE KREMER CIRCUIT, AUGUST 23, 1977. THE CIRCUIT, A FIGURE EIGHT AROUND TWO PYLONS ONE-HALF MILE APART, WAS COMPLETED IN SIX MINUTES, TWENTY-TWO SECONDS. THE PLANE WAS DESIGNED BY DR. PAUL MACCREADY, JR. AND FLOWN BY BRYAN ALLEN. A CASH PRIZE OF 50,000 POUNDS WAS AWARDED BY THE ROYAL AERONAUTICAL SOCIETY, LONDON, ENGLAND.

CALIFORNIA REGISTERED HISTORICAL LANDMARK NO. 923

PLAQUE PLACED BY THE STATE DEPARTMENT OF PARKS AND RECREATION IN COOPERATION WITH THE KERN COUNTY MUSEUM, KERN COUNTY DEPARTMENT OF AIRPORTS, AND KERN COUNTY HISTORICAL SOCIETY, FEBRUARY 24, 1979.

Facts, Figures, Important Dates

The *Gossamer Condor*

Wingspan	96 feet (29.3 m)
Wing area	760 square feet (70.6 sq m)
Height	18 feet (5.5 m)
Length	30 feet (9 m)
Propeller diameter	12 feet (3.7 m)
Propeller speed	90 revolutions per minute
Weight (no pilot)	70 pounds (32 kg)
(with pilot)	207 pounds (94 kg)
Total number of flights	More than 430

The Prize-wInnIng Flight

Date	August 23, 1977
Place	Shafter Airport, near Bakersfield, California
Distance flown	1.15 miles (1.84 m)
Time flown	6 minutes, 22.5 seconds
Average speed	10.82 miles (17.31 km) per hour

For Further Reading

Boyne, Walter J. *The Smithsonian Book of Flight for Young People.* New York: Atheneum, 1988.

Hook, Jason. *Twenty Names in Aviation.* New York: Marshall Cavendish, 1990.

McMullen, David and Susan McMullen. *First into the Air: The First Airplanes.* New York: C.P.I. Publishing, Inc., 1978.

The Visual Dictionary of Flight. New York: Dorling Kindersley, 1992.

Audiovisual

E.I. du Pont de Nemours & Co. *Gossamer Albatross.* Studio City, CA: Twin Tower Enterprises, 1987. Video cassette (VHS) release of the 1980 motion picture.

Index

About the Author

Richard L. Taylor is an Associate Professor Emeritus in the Department of Aviation at the Ohio State University, having retired in 1988 after twenty-two years as an aviation educator. At retirement, he was the Director of Flight Operations and Training, with responsibility for all flight training and university air transportation. He holds two degrees from Ohio State University: a B.S. in Agriculture and an M.A. in Journalism.

His first aviation book, *Instrument Flying,* was published in 1972, and continues in its third edition as one of the best-sellers in popular aviation literature. Since then, he has written five more books for pilots, and hundreds of articles and columns for aviation magazines.

Taylor began his aviation career in 1955 when he entered U.S. Air Force pilot training, and after four years on active duty continued his military activity as a reservist until retirement as a Major and Command Pilot in 1979.

Still active as a pilot and accident investigator in addition to his writing, Taylor flies frequently for business and pleasure. Mr. Taylor's books for Franklin Watts include *First Flight, The First Solo Flight Around the World, The First Flight Across the United States, The First Supersonic Flight, The First Solo Transatlantic Flight,* and *The First Transcontinental Air Service.* He and his wife, Nancy, live in Dublin, a suburb of Columbus, Ohio.